A Wilderness Trilogy
THE OLYMPICS

A PHOTOGRAPHIC JOURNEY WITH

ROSS HAMILTON

WRITTEN BY

JANET SCHARF

PUBLISHED BY

ROSS HAMILTON PHOTOGRAPHY, INC.

This book is dedicated to my parents who taught me to see...
Mildred and Oliver Hamilton.

ROSS HAMILTON's work has been published in many forms, including magazines, books, videos and cards. His long and passionate pursuit of wilderness photography has earned him the reputation of being both a master of his subject and his art. Many enjoyable years have been spent sharing this knowledge with others in slide presentations, seminars and college level classes. His greatest joy is found in the field, recording the beauty around him for others to enjoy.

JANET SCHARF, author and photographer, has hiked extensively throughout the Olympic Peninsula. Her work at Olympic National Park spans several decades, first as district naturalist and currently as the exhibits and publications specialist. Janet creates visitor center, ranger station and children's discovery room exhibits and writes interpretive publications, including a pictorial book about Olympic National Park that is published in several languages. She earned a Bachelor of Arts degree in anthropology and a Master of Science degree in botany from the University of California.

Made possible by the generous funding of Bill Littlejohn.

Published by Ross Hamilton Photography, Inc.
P.O. Box 179, Sequim, WA 98382 USA

© 2007   Third printing 2007

Library of Congress Catalog Card Number 2001116667
ISBN 0-9708154-0-9, Softbound
ISBN 0-9708154-1-7, Hardbound
Printed in Korea

Book production and cover design by Ruth Marcus, Sequim, WA.

Map of the Olympic Peninsula reproduced with permission
by Raven Maps & Images, Medford, OR 97501.

CONTENTS

ARTIST'S STATEMENT

The natural splendor of the Olympic Peninsula eclipses human creativity. My passion has been not to create but to honor the creation I have found here.

This journey celebrates 30 years of time and tide, wind and weather, season and circumstance. The capriciousness of these elements often made long waits futile and the prizes elusive. Unfortunately, much of the ambience is lost in still photography—bird songs, water music, the aromas of balsam fir and flowering fields of lupine, the warmth of the sun, the cold of northwest rains. But I hope enough of the excitement of the moment seeps through these images to convey the richness of this remarkable place.

I have had the privilege of hiking many of the Peninsula's 900 miles of trail, using countless rolls and sheets of film (both 35mm and 4" x 5") to record my discoveries. I could not have done it alone. I am deeply indebted to many tolerant souls, among whom are my friends in the venerable Klahhane Club who didn't mind me making it late to camp and Dr. and Mrs. Richard VanCalcar, who cheerfully backpacked heavy loads for days to reach remote locations. And now, thanks to the encouragement and financial support of Bill Littlejohn, this book has become a reality.

Finally, homage must be given to the Creator of this wilderness. May our discoveries of His artistry and wisdom bring us all to a place of wonder.

— Ross Hamilton

PROLOGUE

Enter the Olympics and its showcase of waters will enchant you. From mist and ice to tidepools and torrents, water relentlessly shapes and sustains the Olympic Peninsula. More than 1,400 square miles of this rain-enriched Peninsula are preserved in Olympic National Park.

Rain falls earthward, splashes outward and saturates everything in its path. Precipitation is measured in feet, not inches, with 12 to 15 feet of water drenching west side rain forest valleys each year. This abundant moisture nurtures a diversity of wildlife, from Roosevelt elk to banana slugs.

In contrast, the northeast corner of the Peninsula lies in a rain shadow. Sequim Prairie, with only 15 inches of rain a year, actually supports a native cactus.

Hundreds of miles of shoreline border the Peninsula, including 60 miles of wild Pacific coast protected in Olympic National Park. Fierce rain-soaked waves pound the outer coast, while quiet ripples shape inland shores.

Dotting the Peninsula are glacial lakes, from tarns to 600-foot deep cauldrons, that truly shine like gems in the rough. Rivers radiate from the central mountain core and deepen its major valleys, many of which are glacier-formed. These waterways provide important routes for anadramous fish, including coho salmon and steelhead trout that swim from natal rivers to the sea and return home to spawn.

Snow tantalizes the lowlands and piles up on mountains, with storms tossing over 100 feet of snowfall on Mount Olympus each year. Throughout the Olympic massif, more than 60 glaciers continuously carve the alpine landscape.

Often unique, always splendid, the Olympic Peninsula offers a place to climb sky-tinted glaciers or experience a fireworks sunrise over inland waters. So lace up your boots, grab your pack and let's explore the Olympic trilogy—coast, forest and mountains.

Fortress of water
Stopping the earthgrow
Shifting the sandflow
Year after year.

Ancient formations
Encircled by surf sounds
Wave-contoured columns
Meld with the sea.

Paint-tinted tide life
Nestled in rock homes
Sensing the sea moves
Eternally free.

All the sea's wisdom
Blessed by life's magic
Memories of journeys
Shared with those dear.

The Coast

Afternoon sun casts a fleeting glow upon Rialto Beach, where the Peninsula's western shore is the essence of wilderness. Here, nothing stands between you and the vast sea. Nothing but breezes, bald eagles and bountiful dreams.

Along northern and eastern stretches of the Peninsula, the Strait of Juan de Fuca and Hood Canal capture the cadence of the Northwest. Scoured out by ancient glaciers, they provide passage for deep-water vessels and playgrounds for sea mammals. Scores of birds find seasonal and permanent homes along these cold and copious waterways where life touches magic.

When morning steps quietly over Olympic's shores, stillness listens. Wood ducks skim over night-nestled waters. Animal families forage for food amid rivers and rushes. Soon the day takes center stage. Migrating whales charge the waves while fine-legged sand creatures scuttle. Then skies darken and twilight tiptoes in subtle hues, signaling the rhythm of the night to begin. The tempo is different and characters change, but the timeless performance of life continues. Will you join the dance?

A geologic jumble garnishes the shores of Miller Peninsula along the Strait of Juan de Fuca. Defined, displayed and rearranged by the forces of waves, the origin of each rock is a story in itself. Ice Age glaciers flowed from the north, carving troughs that later became the Peninsula's inland waterways. When these massive ice sheets receded, glacial till remained in their wake. Today, Olympic's radiating riverways add to the collection of coastal stones.

From the Olympic Peninsula, clear views of distant Mount Rainier remain a Northwest rarity. Watery moats of Hood Canal and Puget Sound, celebrated recreational sites and vital passages to sea, frame this volcanic peak. Snow shrouds its 14,411-foot flanks year-round, providing magestic vistas for mariners.

At the end of a wild ride, Duckabush River rests and mingles its long-distance waters with Hood Canal. This nutrient-rich estuary supports harbor seals, Canada geese, trumpeter swans and curious kayakers.

Full of grace, Pacific madrones grow
along Discovery Bay, a setting
with requisite sun and rocky soil.
These broad-leaved evergreen trees
peel to reveal bright new bark.

Dungeness Spit, the longest natural spit in the Northern Hemisphere, stretches five and one-half miles and narrows to fifty feet. Protected in Dungeness National Wildlife Refuge, this unique formation provides a landing strip for over 250 bird species. More than four dozen different land and marine mammals enhance this slender shore of biodiversity.

Morning sun backlights Mount Baker and spreads its glorious gold over Dungeness Bay. Along the sandy shoreline, a driftwood monument stands sentry as it has for 100 years.

Discovery Bay closes the day with crimson splendor. ▶

Salmonberry sunrise tints the San Juan Islands. Awash in the historic straits of Juan de Fuca, Haro, Rosario and Georgia, these watercolor islands send us postcards from the past.

Sequim Bay harbors the moon while earthlight lingers. ▶

At Second Beach, wilderness and weather hold sway.

Whipped into shape by coastal winds, a solitary Sitka spruce withstands immense odds. Morning bird circles nearby, surveying a segment of Olympic National Park's shore. ▶

The shattered water made a misty din.
Great waves looked over others coming in,
And thought of doing something to the shore
That water never did to land before.

—Robert Frost

Amid sea and seastacks at Tunnel Island, we witness the exchange of primeval secrets. Faithful waves erode softer sections of standing rock, returning uplifted ocean floor sediments to their ancient seabeds.

Courted by coastal fog, Second Beach offers timeless reflections. Northwest Indians, with lifestyles shaped by moods of the sea, have shared nearby sands for millennia. ▶

Perennial kelp tangles itself into cast bronze art. Forty-foot stalks grow in dense offshore forests, which shelter and sustain a myriad of marine organisms. Sea otters bob amid buoyant beds of these lanky brown algae and dive for sea urchins that devour the kelp.

Sea foam floats on the sands of Ozette. What other treasures might the tides toss in? ▶

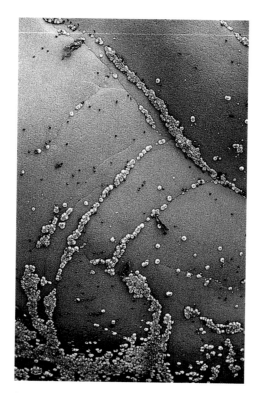

Rhythm strikes a graceful beat
along Olympic's north wilderness
coast. Ribbons of barnacles colonize
creases in sea-scrubbed boulders.
Silhouetted on the horizon,
Father and Son sea stacks rise
from the ocean to share their
sands with each crashing wave.

◄ Toleak Point beckons backpackers. At any moment, a Steller's sea lion, sea otter or gray whale might punctuate this seemingly still arena.

I must go down to the seas again,
for the call of the running tide
Is a wild call and a clear call
that may not be denied;
And all I ask is a windy day
with the white clouds flying
And the flung spray and
the blown spume,
and the sea-gulls crying.

— John Masefield

Ancient icons at Point of the Arches tell a story of persistence and change. Beneath their feet thrives a wonderful mix of sculpins and sea urchins that vie for food from the incoming tides.

The world's largest and fastest seastar is also the most feared tidepool predator. Living in the low tide zone of the Peninsula's rocky northwest shores, the sunflower star grows over three feet wide and sports more than twenty-four arms. This star steals the show!

Giant green anemones, pigmented with populations of minute green algae, share the submerged low tide zone. In the middle tide zone, covered by saltwater twice a day, ochre sea stars configure the lower levels of mussel habitat. With its tube feet and extrusive stomach, a hungry sea star collects and digests mussel morsels.

Will Point protects a deep,
secluded bay. Sea birds rest here
to strategize their next Pacific patrol.

Azure skies work their alchemy
on tempestuous seas south of
Taylor's Point.

I always leave this primitive beach reluctantly. The music of the oceanfront seems to establish a rhythm in man. For hours and even days afterward I can almost hear the booming of the tides on the headlands and the sound of the wind in the giant spruce.

— Justice William O. Douglas
about Olympic's wild coast

Softly the rain falls
Twining like amber
Falling through freedoms
Nestled in gold.

Surrounded by verdant
Layers of leaf flow
Stacked upon moss glow
Fresh from the dew.

Gentle beginnings
Petals unfolding
Finding some sunlight
Filtering through.

Look for resurgence
Find its emotion
Under a leaf-like
Tree that grows old.

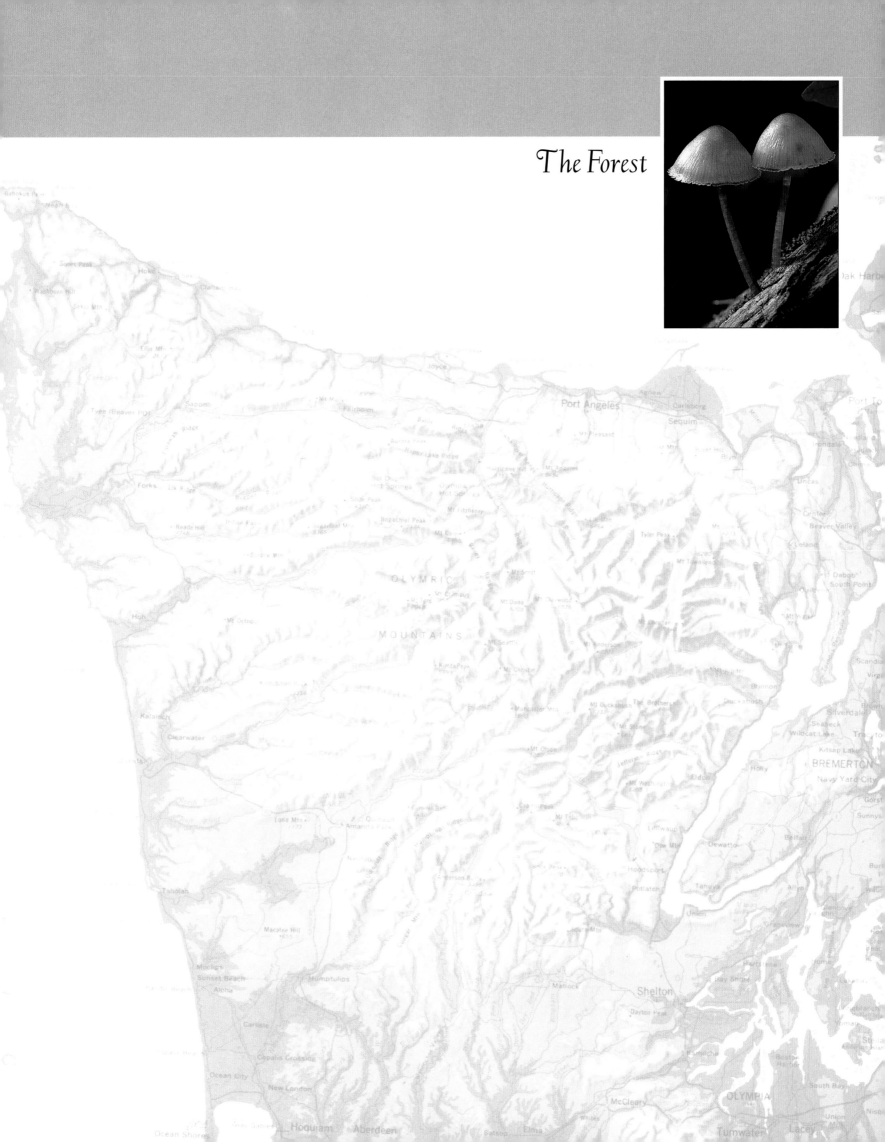

The Forest

Green floats. In the air, amid branches, around trunks. Like a lustrous stone, the Hoh Valley emits shades of jade year-round.

The temperate rain forest on the Peninsula's west side may reach heights of 300 feet with western hemlock, Sitka spruce, Douglas-fir and western redcedar trees. Luxuriant groundcover envelopes every boulder and fallen log. Curtains of epiphytes hang from bigleaf maples. On the drier east side, the lowland forest displays a different look. Vegetation is less profuse, shamrock-like oxalis becomes scarce and grand fir replaces Sitka spruce.

As you climb nearly a mile high, lowland trees meld into montane forest, which becomes the subalpine community at a median elevation of 4,000 feet. In this exposed environment, it might take a century for a subalpine fir to grow 20 feet tall.

Elusive wildlife fly, dig, chew and browse their way through the Peninsula's forests. Many animals, like cougar and black bear, inhabit all elevations. Others, including mountain-dwelling Olympic marmots, remain in one region throughout their lives. Several species migrate seasonally from one area to another, such as Roosevelt elk, which may summer up and winter down.

From soil to seedling to spire to soil, this loop of life eternalizes Olympic's forests and brings constancy to a world of change. With good stewardship today, our progeny will have the opportunity to protect the trees their ancestors embraced. Let us treasure the forest. Let us celebrate its life.

*The clearest way into the Universe
is through a forest wilderness.*

— John Muir

Triple trilliums usher in spring.

◁ Sun filters through the Sol Duc old-growth forest. People and nature interface in this historic river valley. A century ago, visitors boated across Lake Crescent via paddlewheeler, then rode Stanley Steamers to the original grand hot springs resort.

Lady fern leaflets lift art to its highest level.

◁ Templates of time, evergreen trees stand tall amid fountains of sword ferns. Strength, spirit and serenity commune in the Elwha Valley.

Cascading waters choreograph
the Falls Creek grand finale.
Splashing into Goodman Creek
estuary, forest tributaries mix with
swelling tides from the sea.

Puffballs and a parasol? Thousands of fascinating fungi fill nooks and crannies of Peninsula forests. Some fungi network the underground with root-like mycelia. In this mutually beneficial relationship, the fungi tap sugars from tree roots and in turn provide the tree with enzymes that stimulate their root growth.

Sun-soaked sprays of salmonberry, munched by insects and mottled by time, sing the last stanzas of summer.

Dosewallips River erupts into flame with reflections of vine maple foliage. Columns of red alders accent the tableau. Autumn also brings the upstream migration of pink and chum salmon, returning home from their 1,000-mile North Pacific passage. ▶

A painter's palette never wants
when borrowing nature's pigments.

Nature's first green is gold,
Her hardest hue to hold.
Her early leaf's a flower;
But only so an hour.
Then leaf subsides to leaf.
So Eden sank to grief,
So dawn goes down to day.
Nothing gold can stay.

— Robert Frost

Cloaked in antique moss,
bigleaf maple branches reach
out for the surrendering sun
before winter's grip takes hold.

Winter visits the lowlands, dusting western redcedar trunks and flocking fan-like western hemlocks.

Darker yet the forest grows
more slowly as it cools its toes.

Snow sequesters mountains that loom above Heart O' the Hills. The parade of life freezes in formation, except for the occasional snowshoer or snowshoe hare.

The way a crow
Shook down on me
The dust of snow
From a hemlock tree

Has given my heart
A change of mood
And saved some part
Of a day I had rued.

— Robert Frost

Spring sneaks in and frames
Lake Crescent with red alder catkins.
Once afloat, these floral tassels attract
Beardslee and Crescenti trout,
two landlocked fish unique to the
lake's 600-foot deep waters.

Pacific rhododendrons signal spring along the Peninsula's drier east side. A glassy pond near McDonnell Creek mirrors riparian revelry. There's no mistaking this forest awakening.

Flashing a smile at Staircase Rapids, the North Fork Skokomish River embellishes its journey from mountains to sea. This cascading river, full of winter runoff, refreshes the air and moistens nearby mosses. Rainbow and cutthroat trout dart amid huge boulders in their search for mayflies and stoneflies. Bull trout, a threatened native char, prefer to feast on other fish.

It is not possible to step
twice into the same river.

— Heraclitus
c.540–c.480 B.C

Pacific dogwood brings spring fashion to the Olympics with its showy cream-colored bracts. Amid all the green, this lowland tree fleetingly adorns the landscape.

Bunchberry dogwood boutonnieres, diminutive relatives of their namesake tree, brighten deep woods. Soon their reddish berries will accent fall forests.

◄ At Low Divide, in the heart of the Olympics, Lake Mary shares its splendor with backpackers seeking respite from the trail. Cougars, black bears and black-tailed deer quench their thirst along the lake's meandering margins.

Sol Duc Falls speaks in liquid's lavish tongues. Bridging the ravine, the trail ascends to a lake-studded alpine wilderness. Well-described by Quileute Indians, Sol Duc is truly a paradise of "sparkling water."

Delicate mantles of *Oxalis oregana* grow amid the moss in wet west side woods.

Meeting green giants in the Quinault Rain Forest brings many things into perspective. With over 600 years of life experience, many trees have stood their ground through explorations, world wars and the changing face of Olympic Peninsula populations. Their strength gives us courage, their grace lends us peace.

Primitive plumes of sword and lady ferns decorate the Hoh Rain Forest. With over 12 feet of annual rain, moisture-loving ferns grow in abundance.

Vine maples whisper beneath the rain forest canopy. These delicate deciduous trees maximize seasonal growth by holding their leaves horizontally to the light. Young shoots of vine maples attract hungry Roosevelt elk and black-tailed deer.

In a softly-spaced rain forest, western redcedars stand in a straight line. This magnificent colonnade sprouted on a single log—an offering of life from a predecessor. Someday a colossal "crack" will resound through the forest and wooden tonnage will shake the ground. One of these aligned giants will have left the queue, and in so doing, become a nurse log for its progeny. This new line will continue the circle of life.

When it rains, luxuriant lapels
of lichens, licorice ferns and club
mosses become giant sponges
that can load tons of weight
onto bigleaf maple trees.
They wear it well.

They are that that talks of going
But never gets away;
And that talks no less for knowing,
As it grows wiser and older,
That now it means to stay.

— Robert Frost

Up to the mountains
Glory beholden
For those who listen
To the refrains.

Shadowed by rainfall
Hugged by a cloudburst
Weathered not weary
Captured in glow.

Steep are the lessons
Short are the seasons
Flowering treasures
Smothered by snow.

Rivers with voices
From ancient glaciers
Memoirs are melting
Calling our names.

The Mountains

Dawn awakens Royal Lake, a subalpine gem on Olympic National Park's east side. Frigid air lingers above the warmer cauldron, creating wisps of surface mist. In its reflection a rocky slice of Graywolf Ridge, stone-washed by ice, rain, wind and snow, speaks clearly of the Olympic Mountains.

Olympic rocks reflect the mastery of water and uplifting of earth. For eons, ocean sediments of sand, mud and gravel were compressed into shale and sandstone. Meanwhile, basalt lava oozed from underwater vents and fissures and allied with marine sediments. When the oceanic plate edged toward the continental plate, most of the sea floor matter descended beneath the land mass. However, some marine rocks were scraped off and pushed against the mainland, creating precursors of today's mountains.

Ice Age glaciers flowed over these unfinished masterpieces, polishing mountains and carving out valleys. Alpine glaciers continue the artistry in these multiple mountain ranges, relatively low in elevation to be so ice-bound.

Several endemic plant species live only in the Olympic Mountains, long isolated by glaciers and water. Flett's violet, Piper's bellflower and Olympic Mountain milkvetch grow in rocky crags.

For the love of snowy peaks, pastel petals and limpid lakes, come up to the mountains. We'll exchange greetings along winding trails where no sweeter song can be sung.

Winding through changing forests, the road to Hurricane Ridge starts near sea level and culminates amid Olympic's crown jewels.

McCartney Peak floats above the clouds at the head of Lillian River. Morning light momentarily softens its jagged peaks, which reach 6,784 feet. This captivating view from Hurricane Ridge invites visitors to explore the mountain wilderness.

Along the Bailey Range, life seems suspended in the after-storm. Thick layers of snow will defy summer thaw. The long winter plays a major role in Olympic's high country epic.

Hoarfrost freezes meadow grass into crystalline castles. Subalpine firs become statues cemented by the cold. Winter—the season of silence.

To survive winter, supple western hemlocks bend beneath the weight of snow. When weather warms, countless shimmering icicles will drip from their tips.

> *Ah, when to the heart of man*
> *Was it ever less than a treason*
> *To go with the drift of things,*
> *To yield with a grace to reason,*
> *And bow and accept the end*
> *Of a love or a season?*
>
> — Robert Frost

Come summer, Mount Anderson
provides rugged contrast to the
ephemeral blossoms of subalpine
lupine, monkeyflower and Douglasia.
Icy waters of White Creek dance
around this floral array.

The subalpine stage bursts into bloom beneath Mount Angeles.

◄ Awe-inspiring views welcome wilderness hikers to Martins Park. Spectacular Christie Glacier flows over 6,177-foot Mount Christie, eventually spilling its meltwater into the North Fork Quinault River.

There is more to life than increasing its speed.

— Mahatma Gandhi

◁ On its translucent canvas, Upper Lena Lake paints an impressionistic portrait of Mt. Bretherton. A steep and strenuous trail leads to this fragile community.

To climb steep hills requires slow pace at first.

— William Shakespeare

Monkeyflowers share the pink of summer with their equally bright companions.

Above Royal Basin, faceted boulders remain as monuments to a receding glacier. More recently fallen rocks reveal the ever-changing face of mountainscapes. Color-swatching the meadow, thick mats of red mountain-heather conserve moisture for bouts of summer droughts. ▶

Poking through persistent snow,
a lone lily heralds summer.
This remarkable plant gets a head
start on a short season. It generates
heat and melts the snow as it grows.

◄ Expansive drifts of avalanche lilies
flow through Lost Pass, gateway to
the Dosewallips and Sentinel Peak.

A camouflaged *Parnassius clodius*, in the swallowtail family, dries its freshly unfolded wings.

In the Dosewallips Valley, cow-parsnips stand in ovation to Mount Mystery and Little Mystery. Young by geologic standards, these mounds of bumpy basalt originated as broad undersea volcanoes 15 to 55 million years ago. ▶

A sapphire in an emerald setting, Marmot Lake glistens below Mount Duckabush. In surrounding mountain meadows, Olympic marmots emerge from underground mazes to stand guard or eat sweet greens. Wintry weather will send these endemic rodents into hibernation and cover the scene with snow.

Sometimes beauty slips through without explanation.

Formed and framed by all manner of water, Mount Olympus reaches 7,965 feet, higher than any other Olympic peak. This mountain monarch inspired Northwest Indian legends and stirred early explorers. It continues to entice the adventurer.

> *If that be not the home where*
> *dwell the gods, it is certainly*
> *beautiful enough to be,*
> *and I therefore will*
> *call it Mt. Olympus.*
>
> — Captain John Meares
> aboard ship in 1788

The 18-mile hike through Hoh Valley up to Blue Glacier brings Mount Olympus, and a glimpse of the Ice Age, into view.

To climb Mount Olympus is to place your heart first, your dreams first, your mind first and your feet first. There is no second place on Olympus. ▶

A slow-dancing river of ice,
Blue Glacier continues its 2,500-year
performance. Having reached its maximum
growth two centuries ago, the glacier is
currently retreating. Deep crevasses,
exposed by the stretching and cracking
of brittle surface ice, attest to the varying
rates of flow within the glacier.
Douglasia adds seasonal brillance to
Blue Glacier's moraine.

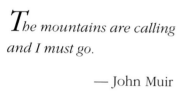

*The mountains are calling
and I must go.*

— John Muir

EPILOGUE

Night moon casts light beams
That swallow up darkness
Illumination so gently
Shines upon life.

Heather voles scamper
And lake lovelies linger
Amid sparkling skies
Above trees that grow slow.

What is that foot noise
Nestled in laughter
Beneath all the night growls
That emerge from the rock?

A moss-covered boulder
Admit we grow older
But better for being
Wrapped up in the night.